Social Media Marketing:
Secrets to Succeed

I0482924

All readers are advised to seek services of competent professionals in legal, business, accounting and finance fields.

You may not sell this product or the any of its rights.

Contents

Tips before You Begin Using Social Media Marketing

Social media marketing is one of the most powerful tools business owners have access to. It allows you to connect with your audience. You can engage and build a community around your business. Business owners can also use it to learn more about their audience so they can better meet their needs.

It's enough to make you want to jump right in, right? However, before you create a profile page and start marketing on your favorite social media site, there are a few steps to take and considerations to make.

Identify Your Purpose and Goals

Why are you using social media and what do you hope to accomplish? There are many different reasons to use social media. You may use it to sell products, to build your opt-in list, or to drive traffic to your landing page. Do you want to generate new leads or build relationships with your existing prospects and clients? Consider both long-term and short-term goals.

For example, if you want to build your opt-in list with social media marketing, how much do you want to achieve by the end of this month and what are your three-year goals? Setting the right goals for you and your business will help you create a social media marketing strategy that's effective and productive.

Identify Tactics to Support Your Goals

There are different tactics to consider based on your business goals. For example, if you want to drive people to your opt-in page then you may want to hold a contest or sweepstakes that motivates people to sign up. You may want to create a content marketing strategy specifically for social media that identifies you as an authority and promotes your opt-in offer. Once you've identified the correct tactics, create an action plan and timeline.

Identify Your Brand Message

What message do you want to convey on your social media page(s) and how do you want to communicate it? Keep in mind that your message and brand should support your other branding efforts. However, your approach can be different on social media.

Finally, assess your resources and leverage technology. Identify the tools and technologies that can help you achieve your social media marketing goals. For example, there are services that automatically publish a link to your blog post on all of your social media accounts. There are also plug-ins that can be added to your website or blog that help visitors connect with you on social media. Use technology to help you achieve your social media marketing goals.

The Basics of Online Marketing

Want to grow your offline business, start a business, or market your services? Online marketing is the way to go. It helps you reach a broader audience, sell, connect, and much more. While internet marketing may seem complicated, once you understand the fundamentals you can build on that knowledge as your needs grow and change. Let's take a look at the basics of online marketing.

Your Website

The foundation for your business online is a website. You must have an online presence to succeed on the internet. It only makes sense. Now your "website" can take several different forms. It can be a blog, a brochure site, or even a storefront. The type of website you build depends largely on your business model.

SEO - Search Engine Optimization

Great, you have a website. Now what? Now you need people to visit your website and you accomplish that with what's called "SEO." It's a strategy that embraces keywords and keyword phrases to attract the attention of the search engines, which in turn help your prospects find you.

For example, if someone wants to buy a new big screen television they might type "Big Screen Television Reviews" into their search engine of choice, Google for example. If you've optimized your site for that keyword phrase, they may find your site and stop by for a visit.

Email Marketing

What does a visitor do once they've stopped by your website? How do you ensure you are able to connect with them, motivate them to visit again, or trigger a purchase? You get their email address. Then you have the ability to connect with them on a consistent basis and build a relationship, sell products or services, and provide value. There are different ways to gather email addresses. You might offer a free report or book that is delivered digitally. You might ask them to become a free member or to subscribe to your newsletter.

Social Marketing

Social marketing involves connecting with your prospects on social sites like a blog, Facebook, Twitter, and even Pinterest. The key is to provide value in the form of thoughtful commentary, information, and sometimes by entertaining.

You build a relationship of trust and authority which in turn motivates visits to your website and/or purchases.

All of these elements are tactics that can work effectively together. For example, you can promote your newsletter on your Facebook page. The key to making them all work well together is to create an online marketing strategy. Online marketing is a powerful way to build any type of business. Learn the fundamentals and thrive.

Advertising and Social Media Marketing

Social media sites have been offering advertising programs for a while now. Sites like Facebook and LinkedIn provide business owners with the means to promote and reach targeted audiences on their sites. The programs are becoming quite popular because of the results they're able to deliver. Additionally, it's a new way to reach your audience and may help you extend your advertising strategy beyond Google.

Why Social Media Advertising Works

In addition to the fact that millions of people access their Twitter, Facebook and Tumblr accounts on a daily basis, they're also accessing the sites on their mobile phone. That means that as an advertiser on one or more of these sites, you're getting in front of your audience on a fairly consistent basis.

Unlike other advertising mediums, it's new so it grabs their attention. Some types of advertising can begin to lose their potency when users become accustomed to them. Their eyes barely glance at the ad before they move on. Social media advertising is new and therefore it's effective.

Targeted Ads

Social media also has the unique ability to market directly to highly targeted prospects. For example, Facebook makes the following statement, "While most online advertising provides about 38% targeting accuracy, Facebook, on average, delivers 89%. On Facebook, you'll only pay to reach the right people who'll love your business."

This is because Facebook and other social marketing sites allow you to segment your audience. You can create ads based on your prospect's location, age and gender, interests, and connections. For example, you can advertise specifically to people who have joined a Facebook event. In some cases you can also find people who are similar to your best customers and create ads specifically for them.

Social media advertising is also generally less expensive than many other advertising opportunities and tactics. You reach more people and get more response from those people. Social media advertising also provides analytics, whereas some advertising methods do not provide this and make advertising efforts a guessing game.

Without analytics, you just don't know if your ad worked or not. With any type of advertising for an internet business, analytics are essential and a clear-cut way to identify which ads are working and how well. You stay in control over your budget and your results.

If you have an advertising budget and strategy, consider adding social media marketing to that plan. You may be surprised at the results. It could change the way your business approaches advertising.

Twitter: One of the Fastest-Growing Social Networking Sites

There are a handful of big players in the social networking world. Twitter appears to be one of the sites that continues to grow in popularity. In fact, according to research complied by Brickfish, as of October 2013 there are 231.7 million active users on Twitter worldwide and 100 million of them log into Twitter daily. So what is Twitter and why is it still growing when many of the other social sites are facing challenges?

What Is Twitter?

Put simply, Twitter is an online social networking and microblogging service that lets you send and read "tweets." Tweets are text messages limited to 140 characters. However, within the context of any tweet you can embed links which makes it a powerful marketing tool for anyone with a blog or a website. Being able to link to other URLs means you can share value and information. You can share links from your own site as well as promote your fellow business owners to build relationships with customers, prospects, and associates.

You can also make your tweets sharable by using the hashtag. The hashtag is the symbol # and it identifies the keywords for your tweet or post. Here are a few examples:

* What are your favorite Thanksgiving traditions? LINK #ThanksgivingMemories #ThanksgivingTraditions
* 10 tips to help you have a relaxed Thanksgiving holiday LINK #NoMoreThanksgivingStress

People can search for your keywords and be led to your Twitter profile where they may follow you and/or share your links with others.

The Power of the Masses

Twitter continues to grow in popularity for a number of reasons. The first is that it is incredibly easy to use. Messages take seconds to write, share, and read. We're a rushed society with little time to peruse long content. If something can be said and shared in just a few characters, we're thrilled.

So in addition to Twitter being easy to use, it's also simple to share messages. One click of a "retweet" button and you've spread the wealth. That means, as a business owner, if you're able to provide a tweet with value and benefit, it stands a good chance of being shared. Each time it is shared by someone, you're reaching a larger audience. One tweet can quickly be viewed by thousands of people. The website traffic possibilities are astounding.

Finally, the folks over at Twitter are continually striving to add value to the site to make it more user friendly and to provide more features. Their partnership with Vine means that people can now easily make and share six-second videos on Twitter. It's just one more way Twitter is providing value and allowing people around the world to communicate.

Business owners looking into marketing with social media may want to take a look at the benefits of embracing Twitter. It's one site that is used by people of all ages and demographics. It continues to grow and provide value.

Gain Financial Success Through Twitter Marketing

Countless businessmen and women have turned to Twitter to reach a new consumer base and generate additional streams of income. The good news is many of them have succeeded in this strategy.

Social media has increasingly become an all-important tool for marketing, with Twitter being the easiest and requires the least time to do. With a bit of knowledge of how to get their attention and how to boost its effectiveness, Twitter could well be the most potent tool you can use.

Provide Valuable Information

One way to grab attention and gain some following is to provide information that has value. It could be something as basic as a famous quote or a tip on how to improve one's life. People are more likely to follow somebody who has some helpful words and can be converted to customers once a bond has been established in the community. You can leave your links in some posts where they'll look good so followers can find out what you're offering. Always remember that spamming the link in each post can annoy people and they can unfollow you just as fast as they followed you.

Use Hashtags Properly

Observe what is currently trending on Twitter and include the hashtags in your post where applicable. Of course they will have to match your tweet, but having a popular hashtag can send your post trending and can be re-tweeted by others which is what it's all about. Using this as a marketing strategy can increase your post's viewership apart from those who are following you.

If one gets off the ground, create another one that has the same tag and add a link. Many people will gain access to your promotion if you are still popular. Avoid following thousands of people with the prospect of arousing interest. Instead, you'll want to increase the number of people beating a trail down your promotional path and to accomplish this, you have to grab attention with the proper use of hashtags.

Don't Overdo Link Posting

On a regular basis, you can post a link to your blog or product site, but don't get carried away. People who pepper their posts with marketing links will soon lose their following as people get irritated by tons of sales pitch choking up their page. They don't want to wade through all that much to find interesting posts. They'll just block you and you're finished. Get attention through interesting posts, and insert your links at random to get more chance of success.

Offer Some Giveaways

Offering some giveaway or holding a contest that will require people to follow you is a smart way of boosting the number of those linking to you. Be nice enough to respond to those who have contacted you or replied to your tweets. They are prospective clients so don't lose time in getting back to them.

Twitter is a potential goldmine if you know how to use it. Don't come off as a spammer who isn't concerned with what people think. Remember that you are building a community of interested followers. Be active online, re-tweet other posts, reply to people but don't overdo the links and the sales pitch.

The Twitter Advantage in Internet Marketing

Many people who are in the internet marketing business don't believe in ad promotion using Twitter because they find it difficult to get their message across in the 140 characters allowed by this platform.

From a marketer's point of view, Twitter appears somewhat negligible on the surface. As an example, you might find out which store someone you're following is shopping at and even the item they purchased. For them, it can be difficult to know how Twitter can help get your message across.

Entry Point for Product Promotion

On the other hand, there are those who recommend Twitter as an entry for promoting their product or service on social media. The idea behind this is that it is easier and consumes less time to reach out to a large number of targeted consumers and hence it is easier to create brand awareness.

Here are some of the other wonderful advantages of using Twitter in your ad campaign.

- Gets feedback on your company's product or services

- Arouses interest or curiosity in forthcoming product launches and promotions
- Puts your skills on center stage and encourages best practices
- Gets you in contact with your followers and provide support if needed
- Creates brand awareness

The best way to move up and forward is to get started and take action. Pay attentionon how your Twitter profile will look like to people. You will need to make use of relevant keywords that can link you to your prospective consumers. Take advantage of this opportunity by adding a link to your blog or website without passing yourself off as a spammer. Since this is a social network, do put a picture of yourself and not a logo of some unknown company.

The Money is In the List

Once you begin to get the hang of this microblogging platform, and perhaps followed a few people, don't forget that building a huge list of followers is your primary goal. If you currently have a list of email subscribers or are involved in Facebook, Google+ or other social networking sites, update your status and invite them to follow you on Twitter.

If you're just starting in your business, you have to try this rather cool Twitter function that enables you to launch a search to discover what conversations are making the rounds in your target niche. Laser-focused niche search – how could you say no?

Sooner or later, you will have a hard time keeping track of your following. Time is gold so you'll need to know to distinguish the essentials from the non-essentials. You can accomplish this by organizing them into various lists using the profile icon's drop down menu. You can make these lists private or private, you decide if you want others to gain access to your list or not.

Tweet or Email?

Twitter gives you the advantage to contact your list of email subscribers which raises your chances of having your message opened and read. With emails, some of your subscribers won't have time to read your email or even bother to open it. With a short tweet, at least your message can easily be read and absorbed by your followers. They can't be annoyed as this won't look like a marketing pitch to them.

Techniques and Tactics for Twitter Marketing

When it comes to social media Marketing, Twitter is currently on top of the list. It is one of the fastest and most affordable ways to get your message across to potential clients and customers. Some companies have only a small following, while others manage to gain a huge number of followers due to the skills they've shown in managing their Twitter advertising campaigns, and discover as a final analysis that Twitter lent a great hand in their campaign's success.

Twitter is definitely not a relaxed and easy form of press-and-forget marketing as projected by numerous social media gurus. And not everyone who uses Twitter is assured of instant success. Hence here are some proven tactics that you can apply and increase your chance of scoring big with your Twitter marketing promotion and maybe help launch your website or business to new heights of success.

Capture Your Viewers' Attention

If you want to grab some attention, you need to plant the seed of curiosity in people. Don't open a Twitter account if all you intend to do is describe how bad you need a fashion makeover or how your alopecia prevents you from approaching the women at your office. Or how you got arrested the night before for D.U.I. You don't want this kind of tweet to go out. It paints an uninteresting image of you and you can lose some or all of your followers or create an unpleasant image for your product brand or service.

Update Your Tweets

You or somebody you trust to manage your Twitter account should make regular status updates. Bear in mind that your followers also follow other people simultaneously and your online existence is often buried under tons of other tweets being posted each day. Only if you regularly update your Twitter account will it be able to rise up and be viewed.

Offer Giveaways or Rewards

You must try to consider giving away special offers or bonus gifts limited only to your Twitter followers. It could be some exclusive item that isn't so easy to find, depending on your type of business. This will give people the drive to follow you, hanging on in anticipation to find out what you are going to say or give away as a reward for getting connected. Unusual offers are a great way to spark a buzz about your business.

Respond and Participate

Eventually, people will be interacting with you on your status updates on Twitter. The best way to ensure that you'll enhance your positive image is to tweet, respond and participate in discussions. This will nurture a developing relationship with potential clients or consumers and demonstrate that your Twitter account isn't just to pitch products.

How to Succeed with Twitter

Success using Twitter isn't as simple as others describe it to be. Many companies launch new Twitter ad campaigns everyday and most hardly make a noticeable impact on the market. To succeed with a Twitter campaign, apply the techniques and strategies described above. Get yourself on the right track and you'll gain followers that keep on coming back.

Create Effective Brand Awareness with Twitter Marketing

Many types of businesses nowadays rely on the power of social media as an effective promotional tool. One of the more popular social media sites is Twitter which is known for uniting an immense number of individuals in one enormous online community. With some Twitter marketing skills, you can advertise your website, products and/or services in less time at a very low cost.

1. Insert Niche Keyword in Your Bio and Tweets

Search your niche for important keywords and choose the ones which you can seamlessly include in your bio. The chosen keywords should look natural. If keywords or phrases are hard to find for that purpose, choose words that are associated with your niche or subjects to discuss. Construct your sentences in relation to these words. One possibility is to add in two of these words as you talk about your work experience or special skills.

Links to your videos or articles should have a sentence or phrase that serves as an introduction for them. It can describe a solution to your target's long-standing problem. Use a personal tone, not a sales pitch, in your technique. Add the keyword that you used in your video or article into your tweet but don't make it sound like you're selling something. Nothing can make you lose your followers faster than this.

2. Ask for Re-tweets of Your Tweets

Don't be ashamed to ask for re-tweets. You hear this marketing tip a lot but many don't put it into practice. Don't expect your followers to automatically re-tweet your message no matter how great they appreciate them. Simply request them to re-tweet any of your posts that they think will be helpful or interesting.

3. Inspire Others

Twitter owners who frequently post words that empower or encourage people to bravely face life's challenges get a large share of Twitter traffic. Let's say for instance that you are campaigning for a consulting company for small scale businesses. Share a couple of really amazing quotes that will drive small businessmen to push harder to reach their goal. You can also post advice on how to succeed in their undertakings. They would definitely want to 'follow' you to learn more.

4. Take a Stand on Certain Issues

Many people are inclined to 'follow' people who post daring statements. Don't be afraid to disagree with the opinion if you have to. However, you can present your opposition without using strong words as they can offend your followers and hurt the brand you're trying hard to promote.

5. Connect

Even if you are using your Twitter account to promote your brand, nothing should prevent you from sharing your ideas, hopes, and dreams with your followers to allow them to connect with you in a more personal manner. You can gain their trust as they get to know the real you.

You can apply all the techniques described above or maybe some of them that will fit your promotional strategies. Bear in mind that constant practice of these techniques can increase your chances of succeeding in the future.

Twitter Marketing - Tips and Techniques for Beginners

More and more people are getting hooked to this extremely popular social networking site known as Twitter. This microblogging platform has become an indispensable tool for sending and receiving updates from a huge number of people. Many enterprising individuals have also used it to promote their brand online.

If you are new to Twitter and are interested to learn how to use it as a fast and cost-effective ad promotion tool, here are several tips to help you start your own Twitter marketing campaign.

- Work on getting prospective clients to follow you. However, from a business point of view, you don't need merely followers but followers who are likely to buy your products or pay for your services. These are the type of people you want as followers, people who are ready to buy. They can ensure a successful marketing promotion once you've got everything in place.

- Master how to use Twitter messages or tweets to arouse the interest and curiosity of your followers. Advertising people who have perfected this art of grabbing attention have succeeded tremendously. Bear in mind that tweets are messages of limited length (140 characters including spaces) so if you want to hold your potential customers' attention, then you should know how to use minimum amount of space to create a maximum amount of attention and curiosity in your followers.

- People browsing the Web for solutions to their problems unfortunately have very short attention span. In this case, tweets are your best friends since they just take a moment to read. However, you need to know what your followers' problems are and how your products or service can provide a solution. Bear in mind that you don't have the luxury of long ad copy. Since advertising space in tweets is very limited, you must be able to compress the benefits of your brand in a few words. If you can grab their interest with only limited space, then you are halfway up the ladder of success.

- Learn to pay attention to people's problems. Most online entrepreneurs commit the grievous mistake of being too concerned on how to market their product instead of thinking of the solution that will end their followers' problems. It's all about what they need and not what you think you want. When they ask a question, you should be ready with a prompt and helpful reply.

This may sound ridiculous but it's true: many people are ready to launch their Twitter ad campaign when it suddenly strikes them that they don't have a website. While Twitter can be an awesome marketing tool, you need to take note that before you can even start your promotional campaign, you need to put your company website up. Your site is where your brand is promoted, and where followers and potential clients will end up after following the link in your post. No website, no business. But that's another topic that we'll discuss sometime in the future.

LinkedIn: Still a Great Source for Social Networking

LinkedIn is a specialty social networking site. It's much more specialized than the others due to the audience it attracts. LinkedIn is specifically for professionals. If you're looking for a job then it's a must. However, business owners looking to attract prospects and connect with industry professionals can also utilize LinkedIn in a productive and prosperous way.

What Is LinkedIn?

LinkedIn is the world's largest professional network with 225 million members in over 200 countries. It's a social networking site that offers professionals a number of benefits and features. It began in concept in the living room of the owner and was launched in 2003. Ten years later it is a thriving social networking site that can be used in a number of business building ways.

The Many Features and Benefits of LinkedIn

Company Pages – The first element of LinkedIn is that it allows business owners to create Company Pages. Unlike profile pages on other social networking sites, Company

Pages comes with analytics as well as an ability to share meaningful content and promote your business.

LinkedIn groups – This feature may be one of the most beneficial because it allows you to join groups that are specific to your audience and your industry. Within a group you can connect with other professionals and prospects to build an audience. Groups support conversations, article posting, polling, and display group icons on your Company Page to further enhance your connections.

Advertising – Like many social networking sites, LinkedIn offers advertising options for members. You can reach a targeted audience with ads that you can test and track for best results.

Marketing solutions – LinkedIn offers a professional membership that goes above and beyond the standard membership. You can then utilize features like their Marketing Solutions program that also lets you create specific messages for your audience through targeted content marketing.

Integration – Finally, LinkedIn is a site that understands you want to make the most of your social networking efforts. You can integrate many social media sites with your LinkedIn page. Integration saves time and maximizes your results.

Creating Content for LinkedIn

It's important to remember that while you can integrate your social marketing efforts, LinkedIn has a unique audience. It often makes sense to create unique content for LinkedIn followers. They tend to be professionals and their needs may be different than your general audience.

People tend to trust the information they find on LinkedIn more than other sites. This simple fact can help you build tremendous authority and credibility in your niche. If you're not using LinkedIn to grow your business or you've let your profile lag, consider giving this top rated social media site the attention it deserves.

Google+: The Benefits to Your Brand

Google joined the ranks of the top social networking sites when they released Google+. This simple, and free, tool allows you to connect with your audience, share information, and even stream online content. Like other social networking sites, it can be used to brand your business. However, Google+ may offer some benefits to your brand that you just can't find anywhere else.

Create a Hangout

Google Hangouts is a free service that allows you to have conversations with up to ten people. You can also live stream recorded content to thousands of people. Google Hangouts makes it easy to handle small group conversations or large scale content initiatives. There are video chat features which means you can see who you're talking to and vice versa.

It helps you strengthen your brand personality and voice. This can be particularly powerful for small business owners who have direct contact with their clients and prospects. Face-to-face conversations build relationships.

Create Circles

One of the features of Google+ is that it allows you to create circles. These circles are essentially segmented groups of people. For example, you might create a circle for your prospects, and another circle for your customers. You can create a circle for friends and family as well. In fact, you can create as many circles as you want.

People cannot see which circle you place them in so privacy isn't a concern. This circle concept allows you to share content with segmented audiences. You can send one message to prospects and another to customers. Segmentation gives you the power to create branded messages that appeal directly to your audience.

Create a Scrapbook

Google+ has a feature called "Scrapbook Photos." As you may know, visual elements are powerful branding tools. This feature lets you add photos at the top of your Google+ profile. You can add infographics, photos from events, and even photos from products or company services. It's also a good idea to keep your profile page fresh by updating your photos on a regular basis.

Finally, Google+ is a social media tool that you can integrate with your other social networking efforts. You can also use it to create events and upload video and other content forms. Use content to build your brand and to reach targeted groups of people. Link to your website and share visuals to help add personality to your profile and build relationships with your followers.

Igniting and Engaging Your Audience

A key element to building your business through social media is being able to engage with your audience. Posting for the sake of posting won't get you where you want to go. The goal is to capture attention and motivate people to not only become part of your business community but to also become lifelong customers. This requires both seizing attention and then retaining it.

Let's take a look at strategies to both ignite and engage your audience on social media.

Identify the Trigger Points

The first step to engaging your audience is identifying the types of content that they respond to. You'll need to perform a bit of research and testing to accomplish this. You can use keyword searches to start. Using hashtags and your own analytics you can determine the popular topics and the content that draw people to your website.

Once you know what they're looking for, try various content formats, topics, and headlines to identify the material that generates attention and creates conversation and clicks.

Create a Strong Platform

Your audience wants to know what to expect from you. Your platform should ideally support your brand and your voice. That being said, you can be creative with your platform. For example, you can use your social media profile to provide a daily tip for your readers. You can share commentary and make your platform one that is primarily editorial. Identify what your audience wants and how you can offer them value, and then format a platform around that opportunity.

Invite Conversation

One cannot engage others without asking questions and inviting feedback. Whether you publish polls, ask for opinions, seek advice or incite controversy and start a dialogue – the goal for social media is to motivate your readers and followers to get involved. This requires a call to action. Tell your readers what to do next. If you want them to answer a question, ask them to answer a question. If you want their opinion, ask, "What's your opinion?"

Finally, be sure to test and track your efforts as you learn and engage. Track the posts that people really get excited about. Track the material and links that generate the most clicks.

And by all means track the material that results in conversions. The more you know about your audience, the more you can provide them with the right material - the material that not only provides value but also encourages them to become an active member of your business community.

Making the Most of Your Website or Blog

Chances are you're putting a lot of time, energy, and effort into your blog or website. Are you getting the results that you want? Are you achieving your online business goals? If not, you may not be making the most of your website or blog.

Test, Test, and Test Some More

The best way to make the most of your website or blog is to test what works and what doesn't. There are many different things you can test and ways to test. Test headlines, test calls to action and test different content formats.

For example, your audience may respond more energetically to video content than they do to print content. Or maybe they prefer reviews over "how to" articles. Testing is the only way to know what your audience is responding to. Once you know, then you can adapt your strategies and tactics. Split testing is often the easiest method to test.

Analytics

Analytics are almost a website or blog essential. They tell you who visits your site, how long they stay there and what pages they navigate to. Analytics can also tell you the organic keywords used, or the link used, to find your website. Google Analytics is a free tool that makes it easy to create an account and then literally cut and paste a piece of code into your site's code.

Just cutting and pasting code isn't enough, though. You need to also review the analytics and base your strategy and decisions on the information. For example, if you find out that the majority of your visitors come from the south then you might create more content, promotions, and offers that appeal to that region.

Facilitate Engagement

If you're not encouraging participation, comments, and interaction then you're missing out. Create systems and opportunities to connect and allow conversation. Blog commenting is a start.

However, the posts need to ask questions and motivate responses. Even more, you want to reply to comments in a thoughtful manner that motivates more comments and feedback. Plug-ins that create forums, chats, and social media participation are another means to facilitate engagement.

To make the most of your website or blog, you want to create a stronger connection with your audience and visitors. By testing, using analytics to track the results, and by creating opportunities for conversation, you're able to take your site to the next level. It strengthens your relationships with your audience and helps increase traffic, opt-ins, as well as conversions and sales.

Driving Traffic to Your Website

Social media is a fantastic tool to help start conversations with prospects and customers. However, if those customers don't transition to your website then you may not be reaching your sales and marketing goals. A few tweaks to your social media strategy may help you gain the traffic you desire.

#1 Make Your Content Searchable

Sites like Twitter allow you to include tags in your posts, aka hashtags#. Pinterest allows you to identify categories and include tags. Use these features in your post so that your prospects can readily find your information. This simple tactic will help attract more people to your social media profile and subsequently more people to your website.

#2 Obvious Contact Information

You might be surprised how many business owners have social media pages and profiles but their website address is a real challenge to find. It's a simple thing; make sure your URL, email address, and even your phone number are on your site. Be completely transparent so prospects feel comfortable trusting you. Additionally, the more obvious your URL is, the more likely a prospect is to click on it and visit your website.

#3 Incentivize

Give your social media followers a reason to visit your website. Host a special promotion for them. Give something away,or hold a contest or sweepstakes. For example, you might offer a printable coupon for Facebook followers only. In your promotion, include a link to the promotional page.

#4 Value Driven

Before you post anything on any social media site, make sure it provides value to your audience. If it doesn't have a clear benefit, don't post it. That means often keeping personal posts and business posts separate – unless your personality and personal life are relevant to your brand.

Test and track your posts to identify which posts generate the most traffic and interest. Also consider including a call to action and a link in some of your posts, and test and track those as well.

#5 Tease

Some social media posts should lead directly to your website or blog. Include a few sentences teaser on your social media page and a link to read more. You can do this on any of the social media sites, from 140 characters on Twitter to tantalizing paragraphs on LinkedIn, Google+, and Facebook.

There are dozens of tactics for using social media to drive prospects to your website. At the end of the day it requires two key steps. The first is to make sure you're providing value to your prospects. The second is to test and track your result so you know what works.

Tools to Attract More Life into Your Business

Businesses, like everything else, need a refresher once in a while. If you haven't updated your business or added new features and benefits to your website, it may be time. Often simple steps can help you attract more life into your business.

Video

The majority of business owners share an occasional video. However, by creating a video channel on YouTube or Vine you can reach a new audience and add some life to your business. You can even use short video messages on your sales and landing pages to welcome visitors and connect with them on a more personal level. Consider creating a video series and a channel to add some interest to your business.

Membership Features

Adding a membership feature to your business model and your website can help you build a community. Membership can be free and provide a number of different features and benefits.

For example, you can use a membership to share more

content or more product offers and promotions. You can use a membership to help your prospects and customers connect with each other, ask questions, and build relationships.

You can also use it as a means to provide a little more value to those who take the time and energy to join. There are a number of plug-ins that you can use to add membership to your blog or website.

Mobile Applications

More and more people are buying smart phones. As this trend grows, so too does the opportunity to market with mobile applications. Just about any business model can brainstorm an application that provides value and draws attention to their website and business.

For example, a business coach might create a mobile app that helps business owners track their goals. A virtual assistant might create a 'helpful tip of the day" application. A fitness blogger could create a fitness motivation tool.

There's no end to what you can create. It doesn't have to be complicated to provide value. In fact, some of the most useful applications are simplest. Take a look at your audience and consider how you might meet their needs with technology.

You can sell the application or give it away for free and profit from the advertising. Additionally, you'll build awareness for your business and attract more life into it.

Content, Events and More

Finally, you don't have to take extreme measures to attract more life to your business. You can create a new content series, free report, or hold a webinar to build interest. Look to your audience first and evaluate how you can provide the most value and benefit.